Christmas Piano Solos
For All Piano Methods

LEVEL TWO 2

Table of Contents

T0034037

Christmas Piano Solos Level 2 is designed for use with the second book of any piano method. Some methods may label their second book as *Book 2* (such as the *Hal Leonard Student Piano Library*), and others may label their second book as *Book 1*.

Concepts in *Christmas Piano Solos Level 2*:

Range 	**Symbols** *p, mp, mf, f,* ♯, ♭, ♮, ⌒, *8va, ritard,* ‖
Rhythm $\frac{4}{4}$ time signature $\frac{3}{4}$ time signature	**Intervals** 2nd, 3rd, 4th and 5th melodic and harmonic

ISBN 978-0-7935-8578-6

HAL•LEONARD®

Visit Hal Leonard Online at
www.halleonard.com

Contact us:
Hal Leonard
7777 West Bluemound Road
Milwaukee, WI 53213
Email: info@halleonard.com

In Europe, contact:
Hal Leonard Europe Limited
42 Wigmore Street
Marylebone, London, W1U 2RN
Email: info@halleonardeurope.com

In Australia, contact:
Hal Leonard Australia Pty. Ltd.
4 Lentara Court
Cheltenham, Victoria, 3192 Australia
Email: info@halleonard.com.au

God Rest Ye Merry, Gentlemen

Moderately fast

19th Century English Carol

God rest ye mer - ry, gen - tle - men; let noth - ing you dis - may. Re -

mem - ber, Christ our Sav - ior was born on Christ - mas Day to

Accompaniment (Student plays one octave higher than written.)

Moderately fast

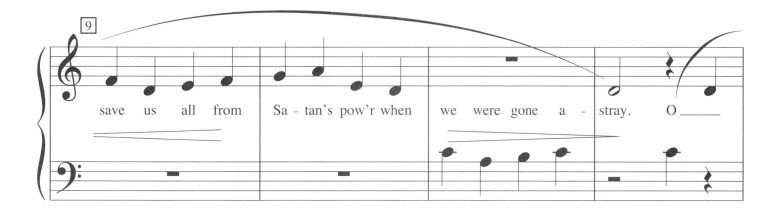

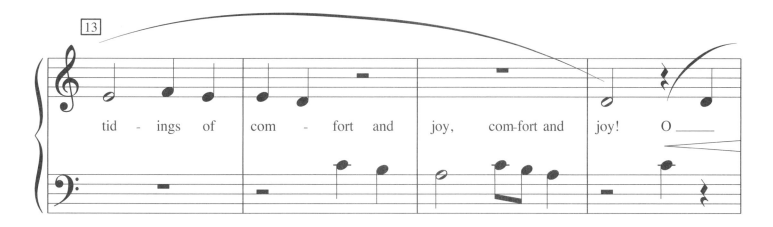

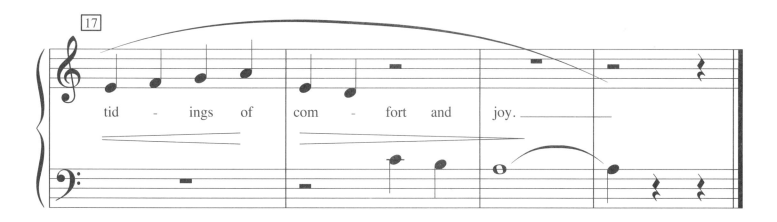

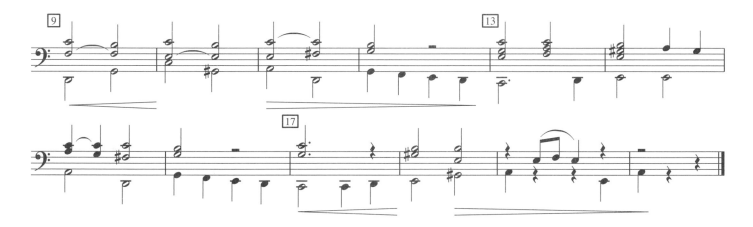

3

I Saw Three Ships

Cheerfully

Traditional English Carol

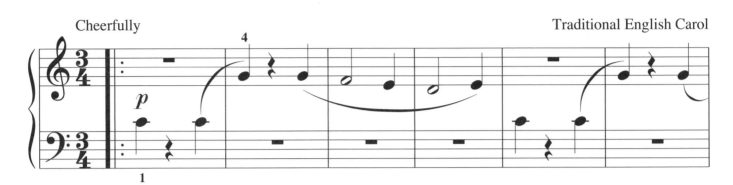

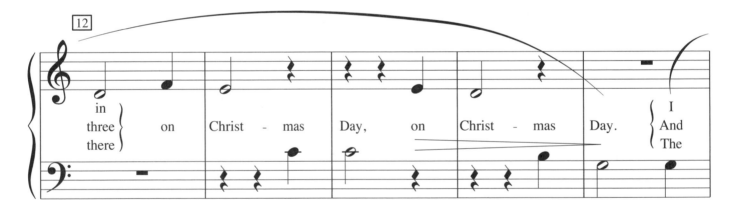

1. I saw three ships come sail - ing
2. And what was in those ships all
3. The Vir - gin Mary and Christ were

in three on Christ - mas Day, on Christ - mas Day. I And The
three there

Accompaniment (Student plays one octave higher than written.)

Cheerfully

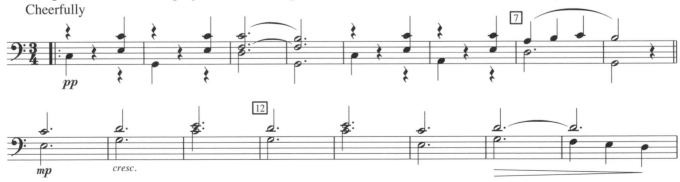

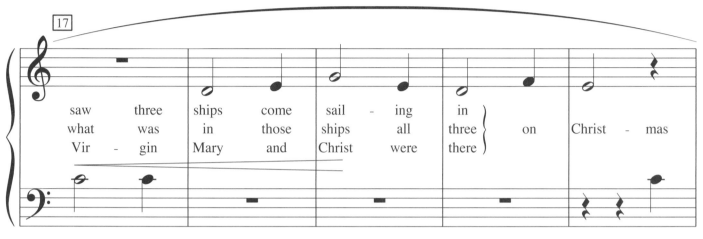

17

saw   three   ships   come   sail - ing   in   on   Christ - mas
what   was   in   those   ships   all   were   three   there
Vir - gin   Mary   and   Christ   were   all

22

*Repeat two times
from beginning.*

Day   in   the   morn - ing.

p

27

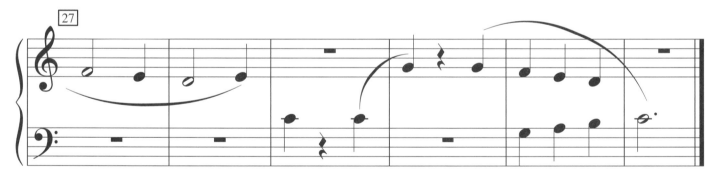

17

cresc.

22

Repeat two times.

27

pp

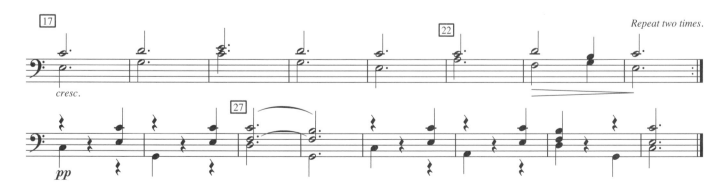

5

It Came Upon the Midnight Clear

Words by Edmund H. Sears
Traditional English Melody
Adapted by Arthur Sullivan

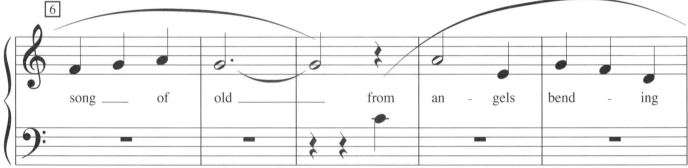

It came up - on ___ the mid - night clear, that glo - rious

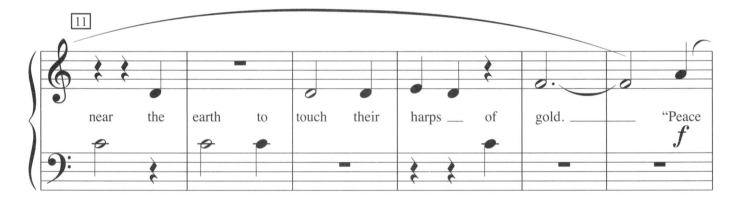

song ___ of old ___ from an - gels bend - ing

near the earth to touch their harps ___ of gold. ___ "Peace

Accompaniment (Student plays one octave higher than written.)

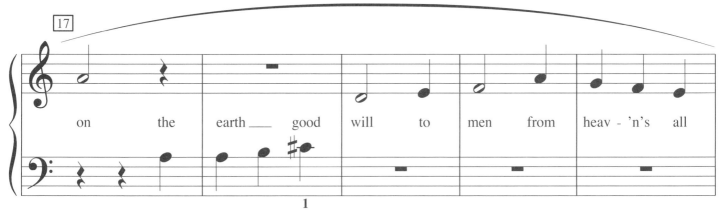

on the earth ___ good will to men from heav - 'n's all

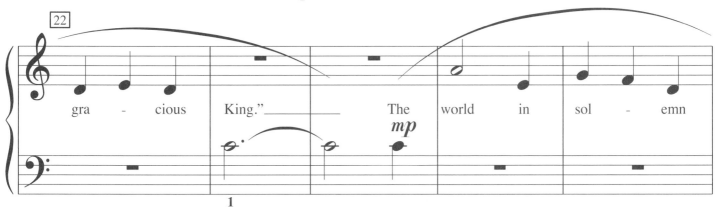

gra - cious King." ___ The world in sol - emn

mp

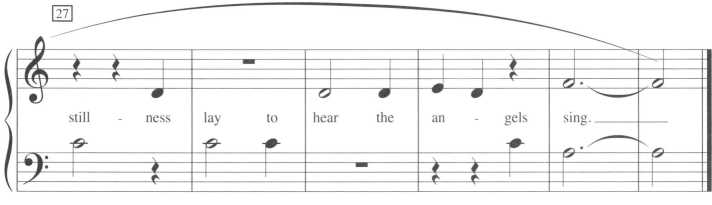

still - ness lay to hear the an - gels sing. ___

7

Sing We Now of Christmas

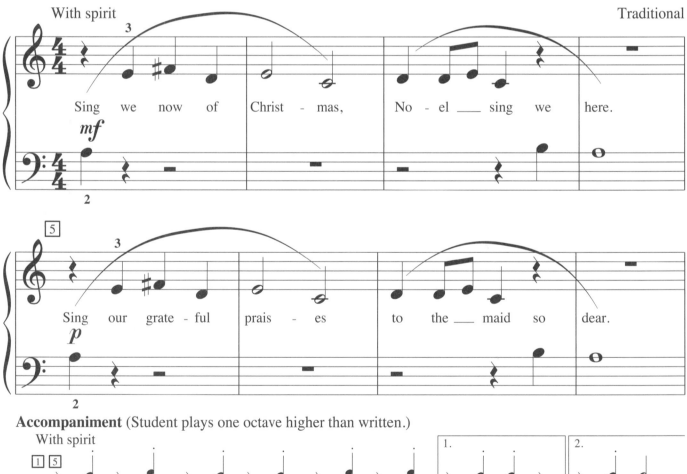

Accompaniment (Student plays one octave higher than written.)

Sing we No - el! The King is born. No - el, No - el!
mf

Sing we now of Christ - mas, sing we __ here No - el.
mp
rit.

both hands 8va

mp
p
rit.

O Little Town of Bethlehem

Words by Phillips Brooks
Music by Lewis H. Redner

Accompaniment (Student plays one octave higher than written.)

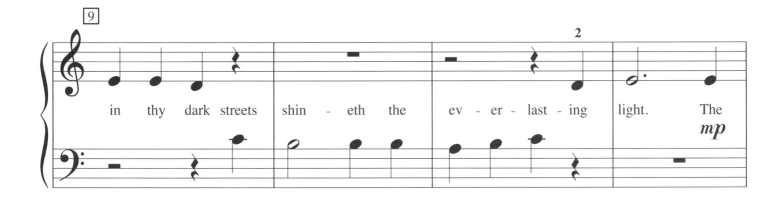

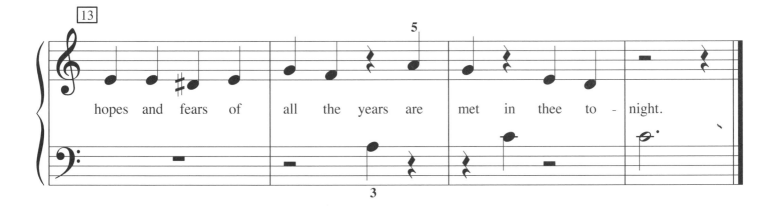

What Child Is This?

Words by William C. Dix
16th Century English Melody

* = student may play ♩. ♪ ♩

Accompaniment (Student plays one octave higher than written.)

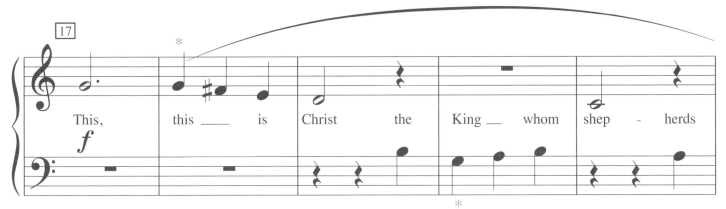

This,   this ___ is Christ   the   King ___ whom   shep - herds

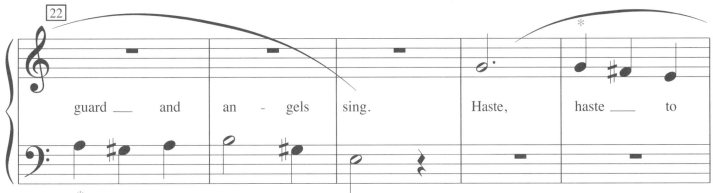

guard ___ and   an - gels   sing.   Haste,   haste ___ to

bring   Him   laud, ___ the   Babe, ___ the   Son ___ of   Ma -   ry.

rit.

O Come, Little Children

Words by C. von Schmidt
Music by J.P.A. Schulz

Moderately fast

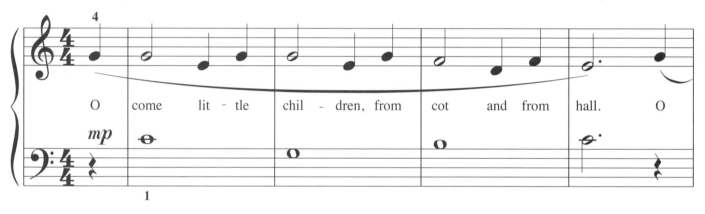

O come lit - tle chil - dren, from cot and from hall. O

mp

come to the man - ger in Beth - le - hem's stall. There

Accompaniment (Student plays one octave higher than written.)

Moderately fast

p

meek - ly He li - eth, the heav - en - ly Child, so

mf

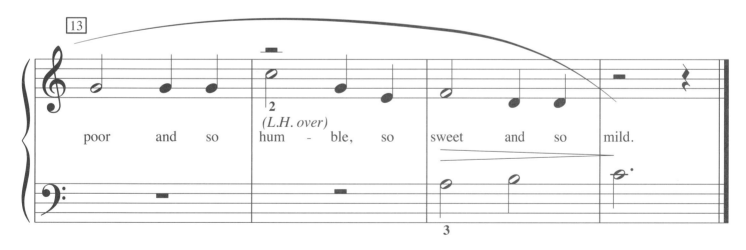

poor and so hum - ble, so sweet and so mild.

(L.H. over)

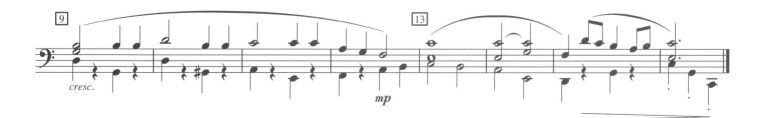

cresc.

mp

Silent Night

Words by Joseph Mohr
Music by Franz Gruber

Andante

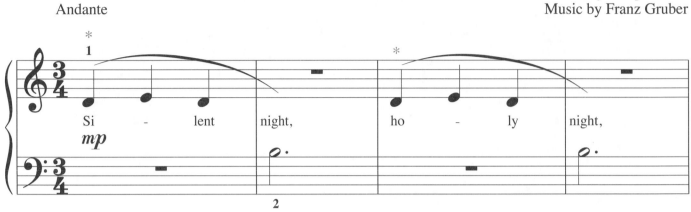

Si - lent night, ho - ly night,

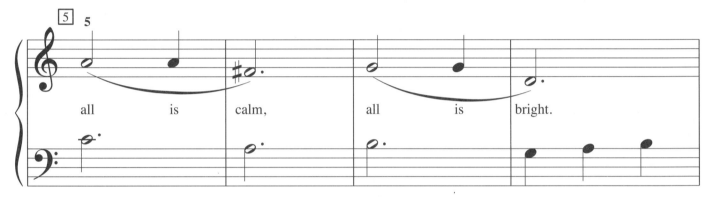

all is calm, all is bright.

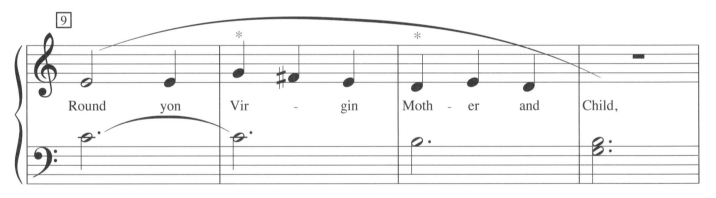

Round yon Vir - gin Moth - er and Child,

* = student may play ♩. ♪ ♩

Accompaniment (Student plays one octave higher than written.)

Andante

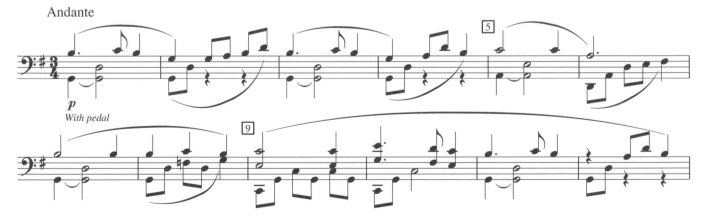

p

With pedal

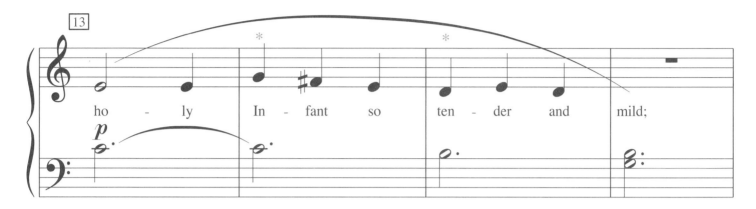

ho - ly   In - fant   so   ten - der   and   mild;

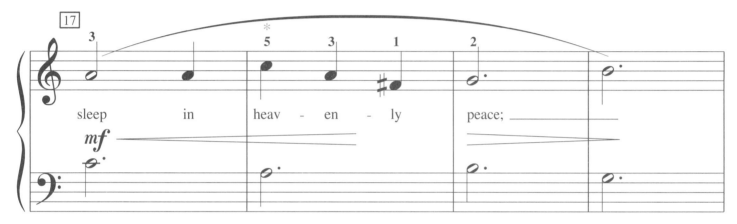

sleep   in   heav - en - ly   peace;

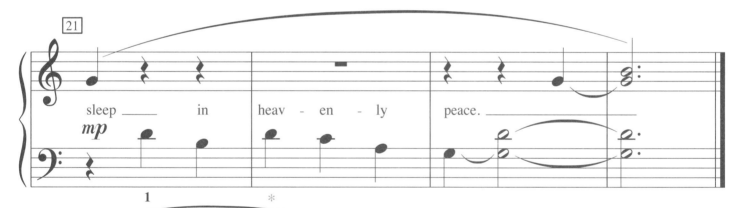

sleep _____ in   heav - en - ly   peace. _____

Joseph Dearest, Joseph Mine

Warmly

Traditional German Carol

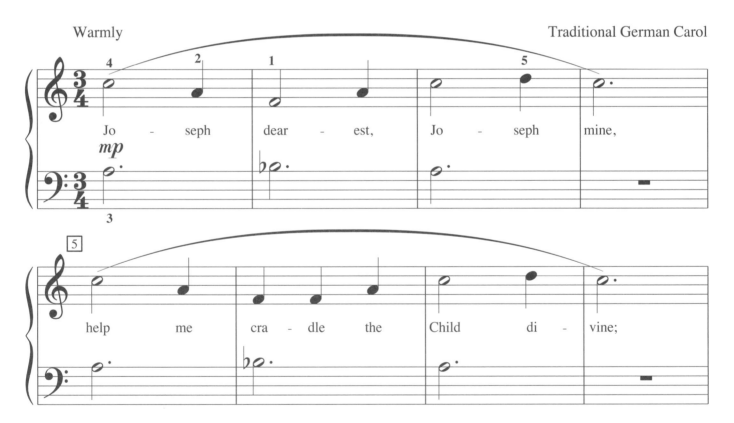

Jo - seph dear - est, Jo - seph mine,

mp

help me cra - dle the Child di - vine;

Accompaniment (Student plays one octave higher than written.)

Warmly

p

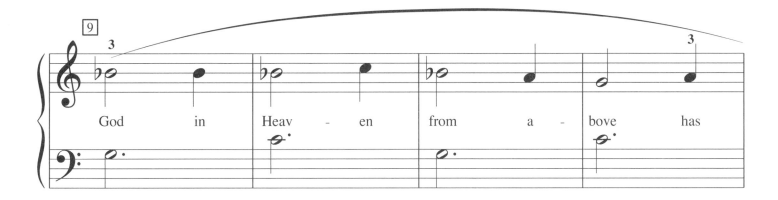

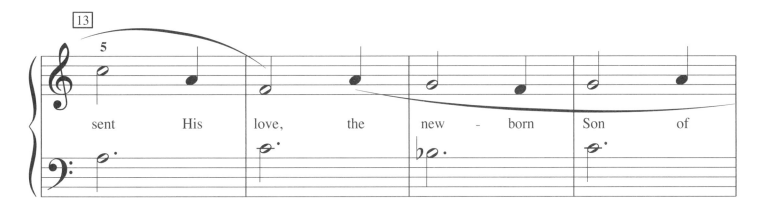

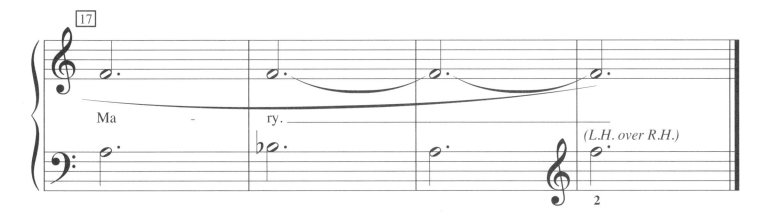

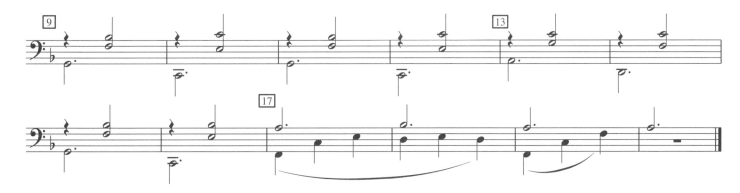

O Come, All Ye Faithful
(Adeste Fidelis)

Words and Music by John Francis Wade
Latin Words translated by Frederick Oakeley

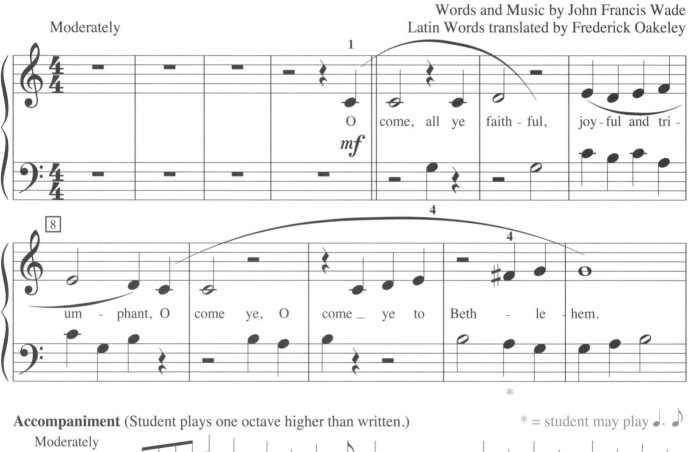

Accompaniment (Student plays one octave higher than written.)

* = student may play ♩. ♪

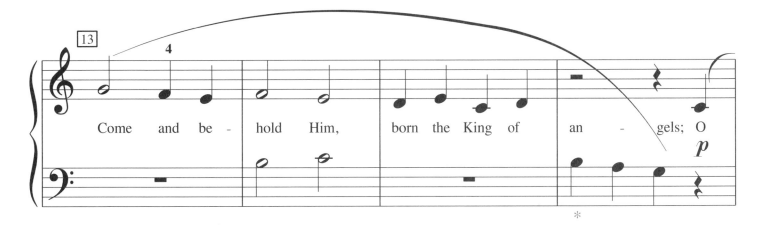

Come and be - hold Him, born the King of an - gels; O *p*

come let us a - dore Him; O *mp* come let us a - dore Him; O *mf*

come let us a - dore Him, _____ Christ _____ the Lord.

Up on the Housetop

Words and Music by
B.R. Handy

Up on the house-top rein-deer pause; out jumps good old San-ta Claus;

down through the chim-ney with lots of toys, all for the lit-tle ones, Christ-mas joys.

Accompaniment (Student plays one octave higher than written.)

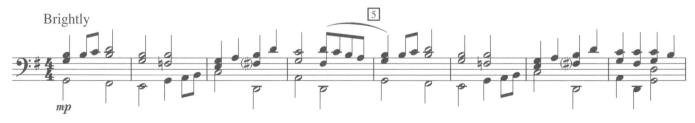

Ho, ho, ho, who would-n't go? Ho, ho, ho, who would-n't go?____

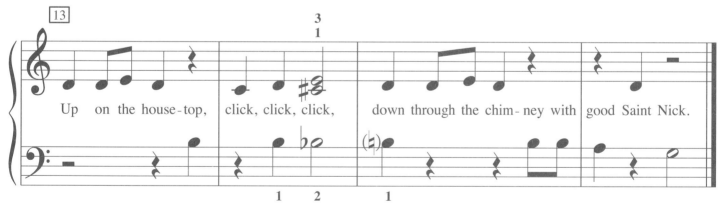

Up on the house-top, click, click, click, down through the chim-ney with good Saint Nick.

Hal Leonard Student Piano Library

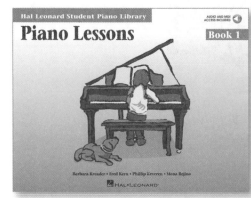

The Hal Leonard Student Piano Library has great music and solid pedagogy delivered in a truly creative and comprehensive method. It's that simple. A creative approach to learning using solid pedagogy and the best music produces skilled musicians! Great music means motivated students, inspired teachers and delighted parents. It's a method that encourages practice, progress, confidence, and best of all – success.

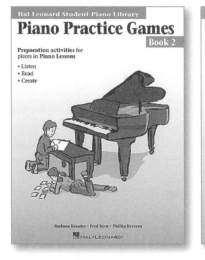

PIANO LESSONS BOOK 1
00296177 Book/Online Audio.............................. $9.99
00296001 Book Only... $7.99

PIANO PRACTICE GAMES BOOK 1
00296002 .... $7.99

PIANO SOLOS BOOK 1
00296568 Book/Online Audio.............................. $9.99
00296003 Book Only... $7.99

PIANO THEORY WORKBOOK BOOK 1
00296023 .... $7.50

PIANO TECHNIQUE BOOK 1
00296563 Book/Online Audio.............................. $8.99
00296105 Book Only... $7.99

NOTESPELLER FOR PIANO BOOK 1
00296088 .... $7.99

TEACHER'S GUIDE BOOK 1
00296048 .... $7.99

PIANO LESSONS BOOK 2
00296178 Book/Online Audio.............................. $9.99
00296006 Book Only... $7.99

PIANO PRACTICE GAMES BOOK 2
00296007 .... $8.99

PIANO SOLOS BOOK 2
00296569 Book/Online Audio.............................. $8.99
00296008 Book Only... $7.99

PIANO THEORY WORKBOOK BOOK 2
00296024 .... $7.99

PIANO TECHNIQUE BOOK 2
00296564 Book/Online Audio.............................. $8.99
00296106 Book Only... $7.99

NOTESPELLER FOR PIANO BOOK 2
00296089 .... $6.99

PIANO LESSONS BOOK 3
00296179 Book/Online Audio.............................. $9.99
00296011 Book Only... $7.99

PIANO PRACTICE GAMES BOOK 3
00296012 .... $7.99

PIANO SOLOS BOOK 3
00296570 Book/Online Audio.............................. $8.99
00296013 Book Only... $7.99

PIANO THEORY WORKBOOK BOOK 3
00296025 .... $7.99

PIANO TECHNIQUE BOOK 3
00296565 Book/Enhanced CD Pack................. $8.99
00296114 Book Only... $7.99

NOTESPELLER FOR PIANO BOOK 3
00296167 .... $7.99

PIANO LESSONS BOOK 4
00296180 Book/Online Audio.............................. $9.99
00296026 Book Only... $7.99

PIANO PRACTICE GAMES BOOK 4
00296027 .... $6.99

PIANO SOLOS BOOK 4
00296571 Book/Online Audio.............................. $8.99
00296028 Book Only... $7.99

PIANO THEORY WORKBOOK BOOK 4
00296038 .... $7.99

PIANO TECHNIQUE BOOK 4
00296566 Book/Online Audio.............................. $8.99
00296115 Book Only... $7.99

PIANO LESSONS BOOK 5
00296181 Book/Online Audio.............................. $9.99
00296041 Book Only... $8.99

PIANO SOLOS BOOK 5
00296572 Book/Online Audio.............................. $9.99
00296043 Book Only... $7.99

PIANO THEORY WORKBOOK BOOK 5
00296042 .... $8.99

PIANO TECHNIQUE BOOK 5
00296567 Book/Online Audio.............................. $8.99
00296116 Book Only... $8.99

ALL-IN-ONE PIANO LESSONS
00296761 Book A – Book/Online Audio $10.99
00296776 Book B – Book/Online Audio $10.99
00296851 Book C – Book/Online Audio $10.99
00296852 Book D – Book/Online Audio $10.99

Prices, contents, and availability subject to change without notice.

HAL•LEONARD®
www.halleonard.com